My grandmother would always
heard, heard and never seen.

CONTENT

- DEDICATION
- SKETCH
- LISTEN
- GOING PLACES
- FOCUS
- YOU'RE NORMAL
- CLARITY
- EASIER
- MOVING
- MY SHARED PRAYER
- ABOUT THE AUTHOR

DEDICATION

hose who settled for what they felt was enough while seeking more and
nderstanding. For those who have expressed there has to be another way but
ever discover the tools to break through.
or those who feel like damn.
ou're giving this thing called living your all but not getting to where you
ant.
hose who are having cloudy visions know you're not alone.
We're going to figure this out together.
We, You, I, Us can and will grow.

SKETCH

23 years of...

- A ton of failed attempts to saving at least 200$ in my checking accounts
- Wore so much camouflage I started to believe most of what I knew was my temporary fantasy
- Running around in life circle with no progress
- Procrastinating until I thought of a faster way to get by
- Going through every emotion within a spiral effect

ile I had put myself through it all.

Why? Because in all honesty too feel important to feel valued and worth it to someone yet alone a crowd fulfills
- Those who doubted you to never underestimate.
- Being neglected
- Getting your heart broken
- Feeling alone on this beautiful earth
- Gives you hope
- Provides that extra strength you might not ever knew you had

Overall makes you happy and I just wanted to be happy.

Knowing no one knows your behind the scenes story.

When I was a little one I remember my grandmother used to tell me to be the best at whatever I wanted to do or become when I got older.

Do you remember growing up and that one relative will find themselves comparing your life progress to someone else?

I was always compared.

I used to live in my shell.

That place of not talking much.
Feeling embarrassed because I felt as if I couldn't get life right.
I was listening, following the directions from the young to old.
I was guarded yet steady comfortable with living in isolation
I wanted to be successful (still do)
I wanted to be the one to change my family in a major way (still do)

But with time and still just growing without a pause on any clock, I could not stop to grasp how in the hell I was going to be my greatest self.

Where to start?
How to get out and show the world I am someone of value.

Listen

My grandmother speaks her famous line daily " Be slow to speak and very quick to listen".

Have you ever reached that breaking point ?

You're sobbing on the floor I mean straight baby sobbing on the floor with snot flowing down your philtrum.
Your vision becomes either black or white solid.
Your breathing turns into damn near hyperventilating.
Every vain surfacing on each known crease from your forehead to your temples has revealed their intertwinment in bold
Your thought of why and how turns into you internally beating yourself up from thinking of all your mistakes.

Do you ever wonder why we go through that phase ?

Oddly after it has all solved itself a cloth of peace or feeling free finally shadows over you.

For me it was one of those breakdowns I had caught myself having an epiphany.

This moment felt as if I was already strongly living amongst it. The vision and details were concreate. My eyes peeled at the grandest moment; I was living a new life while sitting in a walk-in closet. Seeing colors differently, listening to words more of their identity, dissecting conversations, my mind became a built in dictionary/ thesaurus. Any which way a conversation could be perceived I became alert but discovered the true levels of tones.

When was the last time you found yourself thinking of ways to improve?

For your life to finally be wherever you want it?

For that beast pacing inside you, riding your adrenaline to the highest to successfully ease within.

I needed to learn by myself first.
Value myself with or without that crowd, it was then I discovered I'm a dominant human being.

GOING PLACES

Sometimes my personal self can zone out.

You know, just stare at nothing.

My sensory neurons are on break during that moment themselves. It is as if my body went into its own version of computer sleeping mode for a minute.

Has that ever happened to you?

For me it's the strangest glitch.

Because I am unaware of what to expect after.

Although my personal self experience loose wiring at times. I've concluded to expect what I want to expect and accept what I didn't.

Most of us are drawn to this phase when you are attempting to declutter, organize, categorize the many sections of your brain without using a marker or color pencil. In hopes to calm the track star of thoughts in your mind.

Yet, Ever notice once you catch on how your eyes tend to see more, your ears begin to hear even a pen drop and your thoughts silence themselves automatically .

I started naming that feeling Bitch you're growing.

Love it and Keep going through it.

You are now certified to conquer the world with structure.

FOCUS

My personal self on a regular day, I am an overthinker.

I often get this feeling of having the capability to be greater from my yesterday self.

Do you ever think about your day before the day ends?

How much dedication did you put towards your goals?

Were you able to prioritize your schedule ?

Did you acknowledge those who matter to you today ?
Granted time in a day is never regained.

What made today greater than yesterday ?
Whatever it may be, let's run with it and not compare or look too much back
to yesterday.

I should've not…

I would've…

If I knew then what I know now.

elf discipline.

ow much power are we humans storing within ?

hy is it everly exhausting to apply all of yourself everyday?
houldn't it be easy?

Each day you must give patience.

Yes give, because having is meaning one has already retained how to ration out
what needs to be given.
To give, you are learning it's random for every scenario of everyday living.

When you begin your day you have no idea how it may go.
You pray it'll all go well.
You hope the control will remain in your hands.
You're holding on to not failing at any given time.

Mentally your sometimes no longer okay
Emotionally you're not alright
Spiritually you're questioning with full doubt, the alignment of Zen, sanity, peace and happiness no longer exists.
Physically you're smiling. Refusing to allow anyone to see your true form of learning survival.
That pressure.

eing a human comes with a lot.

imply a lot.

udgment colors paintings in every angle

- Social Media
- Music
- Other's views
- Readings

m sure you understand where this is heading

YOU'RE NORMAL

Claustrophobic- having an extreme or irrational fear of confined places.

At some point in our lives, we've all been asked Are you claustrophobic?

Some of us say yes and others may say no.
In some way we are all claustrophobic.

Every day we must choose between something.
That's what makes our days.
It sets our tones.

That's what drowns us mentally exhausted.

We're constantly trying to pick what's best.
Until we find ourselves stuck in the middle of two things.
Realizing there's not much time to choose in a day.

Some things are not meant to be fixed.
I'm unaware of your beliefs my friend, I still respect you and love you but,
for me I believe in my Heavenly Father (my Creature) dropping situations
into my lap just for me to review. To ground me because I also believe what is
fixable you are capable of fixing because he has already provided you with the
tools you need.

Anxiety- a feeling of worry, nervousness, or unease.

We all feel it.
Have you chosen the best?
Or did we fail ourselves?

My dad tells me "As you grow in life, you must shift gears"
To be honest I've always held my breath to do so.

We don't want to fail anyone.
We don't want to appear as weak or lost.
We're not wanting to lose.

Reality you will.
Not just once or twice but through each level of your life you will.
Without failure you won't learn the superior feelings of being tired, having to
be defeated, feeling sick and weak of yourself because you know what you can
do.
Without failure you won't know success.

Depression- feelings of severe despondency and dejection.

After trying to figure out where, how and when to start in our lives for so long.

Walking away from it all feels so much easier.

Have you ever noticed when you're willing to give up everything becomes so much more difficult?

So many obstacles become present in just a second.

eeper questions start to appear.

locking out the world is helpful for some of us.

Others, we need someone to grab onto.

A handful of us may find ourselves coding for help through social media.

Seeking any outlet to bring us back into the sunlight. Take a great amount of courage.

CLARITY

Believe in yourself.

ll you want is pure happiness, to live comfortably,
eacefully while being given a chance to enjoy life.

lthough to get to it seems like hell at times to reach.
ou got this.

You are always at your strongest when you can conquer what we may feel now to be unfixable or forever.

m unsure of your beliefs my friend.
respect and love you all around.

In my personal light, prayer changes in ways I'll never understand, not giving to understand , but I say thank you. Because, I told you before my believer has installed all in which I'm needing to help lead and guide me through whatever I am facing.

In the words of Fred Hammond and the Radicals of Christ
"Late in the midnight hour God's gonna turn it around".
I believe because I've seen.

just want to express from my heart that I'm here with you. You're not
one in any way. Your emotions are valid, what you're feeling is all right to
el. I leave this space for you to just write out how you're feeling and why.
want us to get through these levels together.

-
-
-
-
-
-
-
-
-
-
-

beyond the dots.

ep writing

Draw it out

xpress yourself

Keep going

rite here also

reath...

Think...

Hax...

Release...

Elevate- raise or lift (something) up to a higher posit

<u>EASIER</u>

I was told by a wise individual " You can't pull the carriage before the horse.

Are you a perfectionist?

Maybe an overachiever?

Are you one who prefers to get things done and be over it?

Or you may consider yourself to be someone who just goes with it ?

My personal self, I've tried to tackle everything at once, on the same day. wanted it done so I wouldn't have to worry anymore.

found myself not being able to sleep, becoming more forgetful, losing track
time because I was running my thoughts around one problem.

ot just a problem but, thinking of quicker, easier solutions.

y anxiety reached a level where I was having a growing headache for days to
eks.

I was simply miserable.

From those emotions I would constantly cause myself to face .

I had to learn to give myself time,credit, and breathers.

I began to write an everyday list.

art before the Sun

d before the moon

ediate amongst both

pture during

Every day I look at my tasks, my dreams, and my goals from small to large. Is it crazy to say small tasks, goals, dreams are mightier than large ones? They cause the ripple effect many of us need.

dulting much...

Really take it easy on yourself.

do not want you to go through the misery of trying so hard to prove your
rth that you fall into a sinking hole.

en giving the words of Not Good Enough to control you.

When you look at your list and see what you can take off at any given moment or what can be rolled over onto the next day.

is thing called living gets easier.

om one person telling me to me telling you.

ive yourself a fair chance.

u are a part of a new beginning every raising of the moon and sun .

MOVING

Transformation-a thorough or dramatic change in form or appearance
hen you can see your own flaws, accept your weakness and strengths, take
complete control over yourself.

Never apologize for giving yourself the space and growth you were needing.

Never question if what you've done for yourself is right.

Never explain why you made the decisions you made for yourself to anyone.

Never look back for too long.

Never regret your greatness

emember I said I wanted for everyone to see my value.

t took these words I've clustered together plus much more to understand the
old reality.

DO YOU WITHOUT REGRET!

• Anyone can and will throw you off your course just from them to selfishly take the lead of the life you've wanted for yourself

• In the words of my family who sings this line in harmony.
KEEP YOUR DAMN MOUTH CLOSED !
Don't always go sharing the blessing you see for yourself.

• You don't always need outside Congratulations. Give yourself that sometimes and watch the reactions from others when you do. You'll see who's pure in your life.

MY SHARED PRAYER

Father, I ask you to guide me in the direction you see fits for me.
Protect me, hold me under your wings and continue to lead me onto my path.
 I ask for you to remove those who are not for me out of my following life path.
Continue to provide me the strength, the eyes, ears, and mouth to capture al
of what you're wanting for me as I want for myself.
Father, I thank you. For everything you are doing, plan to do, and have done
You are the Alpha and the Omega.
The King of all Kings.
The Lord of all Lords.
And there is none above you.
Father, I thank you and I will continue to put all my love, trust and faith within you.

ABOUT THE AUTHOR

I'm just Victoria G.

Simplicity is my key

Details I admire

Empowerment I strive to give

I'm witty, with a quirky sense of humor.

Love, Light, Laughter I live in.

Made in the USA
Columbia, SC
03 October 2022

68306764R00048